THAT THE
BLIND
MIGHT
SEE

Copyright © 2012 by Darlene Tucker and Remnant Flame publishing house. All rights reserved

Cover Design © 2012 by Angel Designs. All rights reserved.

Edited by Stephenie Tucker.

Dedicated to My Lord and Saviour
Jesus Christ to whom be Wisdom and Power and Glory and
Honor Forever

In loving memory of the founder of Highway to Heaven
Apostolic Faith Church

Although being my grandfather you were the only earthly father
I ever knew. I love and miss you dearly

Bishop Walter Coleman

And in Loving Memory of living Epistles of Holiness

Mother Matilda Coleman, Founder

&

Elsie Marie Cannon

Of whom the world was not worthy!

I love and miss you both most dearly

"... Write the vision, and make it plain upon tables, that he may run that readeth it. For the vision is yet for an appointed time, but at the end it shall speak, and not lie: though it tarry wait for it; because it will surely come, it will not tarry."

Habakkuk 2:2-3

Table of Contents

Preface	7
Acknowledgements	9
I Come	13
Incoming	15
A Tale of Two Lions	17
Seeds of Righteousness	19
And a Door Was Opened	23
The Prophet	27
Deception	31
Psalm of David	35
Hell Has Risen Up	39
Tabbi's Vision	43
And the Door Was Shut	47
Millennial View	51
The Great Supper	55
Heat Wave	57
Gateway to Heaven	59
Safety	63
Repentance	67
Let Us Hear the Conclusion of the Matter	73

Preface

Every day upon awakening, I find the world an even stranger place than the day before. There is an atmospheric expectation, a battle between the foreboding evil and the great catching away.

Every day my prayer to the Almighty Saviour is to just let me be the witness in this generation, till I find rest in Glory. Like the flower that pines for the sunshine so is my desire to continually abide in His will.

All of creation is groaning in birth pangs travailing for deliverance from the wicked ones. For all creation, from the microscopic abode of the tiniest creature to the sentinel trees of the Redwood forest, has been made subjugated to the corroding effects of sin. Our Glorious Lord is constantly calling out to His Bride to make herself ready. He loves us so much; He has and will continue to send us signs and visions in the midnight hour and dreams at daybreak. He will continue to show signs in heaven above and in the earth beneath, blood and fire and vapor of smoke.

He will continue to use His Mouth pieces, Prophets, Evangelists, Pastors and Teachers to speak forth and sound the alarm of the Coming destruction, to gird up the loins of your mind, to reveal the deception of the enemy and, by the power of the Christ, set the captive free.

This is not a book of fiction; this is a book of dreams and of visions and of revelations, of things to come and things that are happening and things which already have happened, all of which the Lord has shown to me. The Holy Scriptures are being fulfilled on a daily basis, even as it was written, these are the last days when knowledge is increased, "…but the people that do know their God shall be strong, and do exploits." Daniel 11:32 "Many shall be purified, and made white and tried; but the wicked shall do wickedly: and none of the wicked shall understand; but the wise shall understand." Daniel 12:10. Let everyone who reads take heed for the time is at hand.

Acknowledgements

I would like to acknowledge my Lord and Saviour Jesus Christ, my love for Him surpasses all others, For there is no greater Love than His; My gifts from God, my children, Angel, Daennah, Tabitha, David, and Stephenie, who are truly sons of God, whom I love so much and who are my constant inspiration and prayer warriors; My Mama, Shirley Brice who I love dearly and who always believed in me.

My dear sisters and friends in order of when God placed them in my life, Diana Stevenson, Linda Hamlet, Deborah Caldwell, and Myra Robinson who will always love me, I love them the more; My dear big brothers, and body guards, I do so love Michael and James Robinson; My nephews Reggie, Lance, John and Jordan and my nieces Faith, Kee Kee, Krysta, Leah, and my dear cousin Timothy Solomon Lee, all of whom I love dearly.

A million thanks, and much love, to The Boone Family, The Lomax Family, and The Woodards, Mother Heggins and dear Sis Yarbourough, whose prayers always are a constant vigil for my children and me, whom I know are Spiritual Giants in the Lord.

And Dot, who was my one remaining constant in the midst of a time of turmoil.

And yes, Ee, Queenie and Lil Noah, Lil Isaac and Isaiah Bassell sweet baby twins a gift from Heaven, And, Shyah, and Breonna and Myles who will always be so dear to me, along with a host of other Saints, cousins and relatives. I love you all

That the Blind Might See

That the Blind Might See

I COME

The darkness is so thick, it is so engulfing, pressing in; a steady stride of a being. A light slices the darkness, lighting the footsteps of the stride. A clock swings loosely from the being's hand, *look closer,* a voice whispers from somewhere in eternity. Yes, I can see the face of the ominous clock, seemingly alive and desperate, desperate to reach that last stroke, that last stroke of time. I see each moment slipping away into eternity as the strides match the beat of the strokes, each one reaching its destination. The stride stops and the clock registers' midnight. The resounding bell begins to toll loudly, much louder than this small clock should register, *dong, dong, dong,* desperation reaches my soul, *dong, dong.* Suddenly the light is bursting through my eyes as I began to awaken; I hear the Great Eternal One speaking, TELL THEM I COME. TELL THEM I COME.

INCOMING

Suspended in eternity, I'm peering down on the world of time, wearing expectation as a garment, awaiting prophecy's fulfillment. Knowing, looking, and beholding…the destined mountain of fire, targeting the bracing creation. Earth, staggering to and fro, intoxicated by sin, now knocked off its sobriety line by the fireball of prophecy. Fragmented mountain pieces hurl upward making their great escape into space. Valleys give way to gaping holes and oceans are up heaved onto cities and highways, snatching every piece of creation that stands in its pathways. Homes become debris, towns become waterways, mountains become valleys, and many civilizations become graveyards. Untold millions of creatures which had life died.

~~~~~

"And the second angel sounded, and as it were a great mountain burning with fire was cast into the sea; and the third part of the sea became blood; and the third part of the creatures which were in the sea, and had life, died; and the third part of the ships were destroyed."

Revelation 8:8-9

A TALE OF TWO LIONS

A breeze ripples across waist high field of golden grain that stretched out across a rolling field, back dropped by an ancient city with huge monolith buildings made of clay. Piercing intense eyes are boring into me, peering through the face of a goliath sized lion, whose height matches the backdrop of the ancient city that story lined the field. Poised still like a stone god guarding some ancient Egyptian temple, this monstrosity of a body in a sitting position did not register any signs of movement. His mane flowing majestically around his face formed the outline of this beast of a lion, perfectly matching the golden grain of the field. As a grasshopper is to our eyes so was I in his. A ferocious roar bellows out from somewhere within the confines of the ancient city, this gale force roar travels across the golden field forcing the grain to bow in obeisance along with the fluid mane of the lion that stands before me, but monolith doesn't flinch. As the ferocious warning reached my understanding, translation began to happen. Upon hearing the sound of the seven thunders it would be time to flee, flee to the appointed place.

~~~~~

"The lion is come up from his thicket, and the destroyer of the gentiles is on his way; he is gone forth from his place to make thy land desolate; and thy cities shall be laid waste, without an inhabitant." Jeremiah 4: 7

SEEDS OF RIGHTEOUSNESS

Pure white light, so bright, surpassing even that of a thousand suns, forming and reaching, settling into the form of a hand, reaching out towards me, placing gently into my hand the pure white linen cloth, matching that of the garment that is clothing my body. The cloth is now opening, yielding a blossoming cotton seed. A sweet fragrant voice speaks to my soul, directing me to cast this precious seed upon the waters. Astonished eyes looking out upon a still body of water, a hand, my hand, reaches forth in a fluid motion tossing the seed toward the waters. Seed, before landing on the waters, has already multiplied abundantly, some falling upon murky waters, some falling upon the muddy banks, but some falling upon the still waters. Precious voice whispers to my soul, *sow the seed of righteous, some will here and some will forbear, for the time is at hand.* Prostrating now on the floor of my bedroom, heaving sobs of repentance saturate the carpet, I hear a roll thunder speaking somewhat audibly, "Stand upon your feet." Strong gentle Hands hoist me upward and plant me upon my feet, immediately sending forth a line, a diving line that reached the ends of this dry parched ground known as the earth stretching out before my eyes. Wonderful, Marvelous, Holy, Omnipotent *"Be"* speaks resoundingly, piercing asunder soul and spirit, "The Dividing Line has gone out into all the world; it is decision time. Tell them the righteousness of God is the only right choice. Not self-righteousness."

"Upon coming up out of the baptismal watery grave in the only name given among men whereby one must be saved, which is the revealed name of Jesus, upon receiving My Word made flesh indwelling in their souls, they must fulfill my righteousness."

The Resonating Voice, the Almighty which searcheth the reins and hearts spoke again,

"Fulfilling My righteousness will be the only means of placing one on the right side of the diving line that has gone out into all the earth."

"Tell them I come; behold I come quickly, I must come quickly to rapture my people from the wrath to come, from the wrath of the serpent, and from My wrath, The Great

Tribulation which will come upon all the world to try them that dwell therein."

The steady flow of tears is only surpassed by trembling, and glorifying; I cannot be still. I am overwhelmed by His Goodness, His Love, His Joy; His peace is now coursing through me like a mighty river, invigorating every fiber of my being.

Worthy is the Lamb that was slain! Holy, Holy, Holy is the Lord of Hosts; the Whole earth is full of His Glory!

AND A DOOR WAS OPENED

A doorway, or gateway, frames my body; I know not which. At my feet lie wooden planks lined in formation like soldiers, forming a platform.

Beyond the platform lies an embankment of sand monitoring the boundaries of the sea. Beyond the sea to the left, my eyes are drawn to these huge rectangular, box shaped buildings, and overhead dread was encircling the scene like vultures a dying creature. A noise, low at first, a trembling of a sort, rising up from the deep. Screaming and running are island people in fear and torment as seemingly intelligent debris pursues its victims.

The sea begins to rub its back against a foreboding ominous sky, and then overtaking its sand monitor, for it had received permission to supersede its boundaries by the Most High. With a thunderous voice it ransacked everything that stood in its pathway. The metric ton push of waters quickly engulfed roadways so swiftly and unexpectedly that many oblivious travelers literally drove into the broadened boundaries of the advancing sea. Treacherous green clouds began to congregate over the rectangular buildings as the water reached its grounds.

An eerie calm was interrupted by fiery explosions while smoke and fire billowed upward joining the congregation of green clouds, and then the congregation of green and white and eerie began to disperse, moving across the sky like some humongous folklore beast of prey, setting out to conquer what it could of the rest of an unsuspecting world.

A week's worth of time elapsed, unbelieving ears, widened eyes and mouth gaped as the news unfolds on my laptop. The waters coming ashore, the explosive nuclear plants and the radiation fallout have culminated and conspired to make last week's dream today's' reality, Japan. *Warn them, tell them to prepare, for calamity knows no boundaries.*

THAT THE BLIND MIGHT SEE

THE PROPHET

Shadowy figures, edges at the corners of reality. The earth wears darkness as a garment. People are meandering in the darkness. The scene is in alleyways of covertness. Fear is as thick as the lowering midnight cloud covering over head, and the atmosphere is charged with the prophetic Word of a warrior of God. The narrow pavement is aligned with houses that stood at attention like centurion soldiers. The prophetic Word thunders out again alarming, warning somewhere off an elevated attachment of a seemingly reverent home. My Awe struck eyes peering from trembling body, deadlocks with the piercing eyes of the embodiment of the Prophetic Word. The warning cry again rolls off the prophet's tongue "THE WRATH OF THE LAMB IS COMING."

Pointing finger at the end of his ancient arm lulls my attention toward the cloud laden midnight sky. Cumulus nimbus began to move aside in obeisance to some unseen force, revealing a blood dripping moon, a fulfillment of the fullness of time. The heavenly display that captured my eyes in this telltale sight suddenly became the backdrop of the Prophet as he was now standing face to face with me.

The Unspoken questioning words that flooded my mind was met with unwavering devotion and surrender to the Glory and the Will of God. The Prophet now with outstretched weathered hands lowered a gift into mine. I stood Trembling under the power of the Spirit of God, captivated by the reflection of the Great Eternal Wonder that shown in his eyes.

~~~~~

"The sun shall be turned into darkness, and the moon into blood, before the great and terrible day of the LORD come."

Joel 2:31

THAT THE BLIND MIGHT SEE

DECEPTION

Multitudes, multitudes, in the valley of decision. Feet running from every house filling the streets with awe and reverence. Eyes, multitudes of eyes gazing into the heavens, wide with expectation and unwavering devotion; all emotions directed toward the metallic wheel that defies the laws of physics. Many more posturing discs as if on some sort of intergalactic display. Mesmerizing, drawing in the masses, every one's eyes reflecting adoration, undying allegiance and worship. Voices punctuate the scene with echoed elation, "Saviour!" "Lord!" "Jesus!" Fear and sorrow swells up in my soul, pleading squeals burst forth from my mouth, reverberations of warnings pierce the punctuations of elations.

"This is not our Lord!" I cried out in utter shock as my pleas wafts pass the deafened ears of the masses. The multitudes entranced began to follow the now pulsating disc away from the scene and with them my hopes and pleas disappear. Great heaves of sorrows thrust forth from me for the deceived generation. I turn in heaviness and my despair is met with joy. "Come everybody the real victory is here!" I cry. "The battle is over; our Jesus has won!" Great beam of light shattering the darkness of despair stands on the street as an illuminated door. The roll call of a thousand generations beacons from this entrance into eternity.

All Those Who Are Ready Enter In. Translated by the Spirit of God, caught up in a moment; in a twinkling sorrow and sighing is forgotten, and a million years from now, life will have just begun.

~~~~~

"And for this cause, God shall send them strong delusion, that they should believe a lie; that they all might be damned who believed not the Truth, but had pleasure in unrighteousness."

II Thessalonians 2:11-12

That the Blind Might See

PSALM OF DAVID

Bloody battlefield, location: earth. Battle scarred countryside germinates throughout the earth, replacing purple mountains and golden grain. Multitudes of bodies lay strewn about like ragdolls. Untold numbers of Warriors lay still with smiling eyes, not defeated by death. A voice of guidance fills the air, "*The battle is over.*" We, the more than conquerors, led by the Spirit of Christ, gather the remnant while fleeing the wrath to come.

That the Blind Might See

The light in the accumulated darkness, we unquestioningly move on, gathering old warriors and ones who've just begun. Billowing smoke fills the air as fire mars the mountain-less valleys and homeland plains.

Pulling more to safety as we persuade the few to come; van cooperates, seemingly growing larger with the incoming of every soul, as the rotten smell of destruction fills the air.

A deafening roar mimics a beast. Just over the horizon from every side, beast transforms into the towering sea, racing toward us from all around, flooding every heart with fear.

Remnant cries out salvation's plea. Peace replaces fear; despair gives in to hope as tears of sorrow turn into joy.

Cumulous blackness rolls back like a scroll, yielding the way to Purifying Being of Light, The Rock of Ages, The Great

I Am, He that was and is and is to come has come. Remnant eyes intensely reflecting His glory, beast encompasses remnant, launching forth the take its prey, blood stained Hand reaching, holding, gathering, lifting, translating mortals to Immortality.

~~~~~

"Because thou has kept the word of My patience, I also will keep thee from the hour of temptation, which shall come upon all the world, to try them that dwell upon the earth."

Revelation 3:10

THAT THE BLIND MIGHT SEE

HELL HAS RISEN UP

The air is laden with thick smoke; fires are popping up spasmodically all over the city scene that lies before me. Upon entering one house, the stench of death and flames assault me.

"Come quickly!" I cry out to the sleeping, "Come quickly." Reaching through the densely smoked air, desperately trying to grab the now awake but panicky individual.

Finding hope in the midst of despair, I reach the panicked and pull them to safety. The group of escapees is growing as we continue through the condemned city.

Walking and running along the scorching ground, our eyes caught sight of silhouettes plastered against every building, eerie disfigurements and gross contortions of demonic spirits.

Though I walk through the valley of the shadow of death, I will fear no evil for thou art with me. This very verse from the book of Psalms becomes my battleaxe as we proceed to seek and to save those that were lost in the streets of the city and some save we with fear, pulling them out of the fire.

We continue on in this wretched place gathering the remnant for we are the sons of the Most High God.

"For we wrestle not against flesh and blood, but against principalities, against powers, against the rulers of the darkness of this world, against spiritual wickedness in high places."

Ephesians 6:2

"And others save with fear, pulling them out of the fire; hating even the garment spotted by the flesh."

Jude 23

That the Blind Might See

TABBI'S VISION

Lifted up on high, suspended in eternity, surrounded by a gazillion tomorrows. Eyes wide with wonder, soul filled with awe, both focused on the blue sphere of time which rotates below her.

Suddenly, the war cry sounds of a thousand generations flood her ears. Destitution, devastation, famine, atrocity, flashes before her eyes. The floodgates of violence are open, issuing forth monolith waves of iniquity

,pummeling this sphere of time, waxing away the love of many. Monumental clouds of disasters have taken up residence on every corner of the idolatress globe.

The stench of sin germinated from the depths of hell, emanates upward into the heavens becoming a foul smelling savor in the nostrils of His Holiness. Brilliant Light Being pierces the darkness of blackness, descending gracefully and deliberately, stepping down on the wretched rotating planet. Feet of bronze turn into flames, flames of glory, purifying flames replaces Being of light. Being treads every mountain and every valley, as the train of His glorious flames spreads outward and fills this desecrated temple called earth. The earth melts like wax before Him, flames of purification pursue after Him, thousands times ten thousands and thousands of thousands fall around Him. His Glory encompasses the circumference of the earth, until entire creation is subdued by Him. Being, now ascending into glory, leaving in His wake a purified earth, not with the waters of Noah's flood, but with the flood of purifying Refiner's fire. Two sentinels of light displayed in the heavens trumpet out those victorious words, "Behold the Lamb of God which taketh away the sin of the world."

That the Blind Might See

AND THE DOOR WAS SHUT

The terrain is ruff and rocky with marble slabs scattered about. The ground began to shift and give way to long narrow slits interrupting the surface of the plain.

Movement is coming to the surface of the slits; there they were. Swiftly rising from the gapping openings, giant 8 foot picture screens with moving pictures are now surrounding me like sentinels, vying for my attention.

Each screen springs to life with different scenes throughout the planet, in both domestic and distant lands. Left screen, war sounds are blaring loudly with gunshots and bombs exploding and imploding on some foreign land, off some distant shore.

Picture screen to the right springs into the action of ferocious battle-scarred warriors with the battle set in array. Another screen explodes into action with chaotic display of perversion and violence.

Yet another jumps in with turmoil and disasters pulverizing the globe! And suddenly, coming into frontal view, was a display of some sort of forbidden hybrid beast with tell-tale eyes of superior intellect, waiting for his defining moment, that his makers would realize that they are really the puppets and he controls them.

Boiling mass of muddied clouds, incoming from the sky to my left, begin to encompass the face of the whole land. Muddied mass of clouds real identity is horses and their riders, purposefully riding.

Muddied mass of clouds, incoming now also from the right side of the sky, boiling, foaming and reaching, nearing and encompassing the face of the whole land.

Now at closer glance, animals began to come into focus, a ravenous beast of a bear, and pursuing in close range, a pompous lion with eagle wings blocking the view of whatever lies beyond it. *Hurry* the voice implores, *hurry.* Unspoken knowledge flooded my mind, I and others began to gather in, gather in the remnant.

One could almost hear that last bit of sand finishing off in the hourglass of time. We're in now, some were slowful, but still manage to slip into the closing door. Tall, middle-eastern young boy of late teens or early twenties, wearing dark rimmed glasses, just barely steps when the Voice of the Ancient of Days proclaimed "The door was shut"

Though spoken loudly, it was undetected by billions around the big blue marble that hung on nothing in space. Immediately we, the redeemed of the Lord, the ransomed of Christ, were safely hidden in this exceedingly luminous beautiful white high mountain, somewhere north of the ultimate zenith.

A voice rang out, soothing us like a heavenly lullaby, penetrating every fiber of our being, "Come, My people, enter thou into thou chambers, and shut thy doors about thee; hide thyself as it were for a little moment, until the indignation be overpast." (*Isaiah 26:20*)

MILLENNIAL VIEW

Parched weed and grass covered the rolling hills, eyes looking earnestly, contending with obstacles and looking. *Must find the lost, we must find the lost*, overhead a constant reminder of the coming desolation.

Ominous clouds of purple and green are hurriedly approaching, grand-standing the scene, only to be superseded by an emerald green persistent rainbow. Urgency saturates the air. The searchers feet now feeling the press turn toward safety, a fortified fortress whose foundations are deep.

Persistent rainbow steady watching over, guiding us through the ill winds that are blowing relentlessly. Sweet aroma of melodious music satiates our being as we enter the strong tower, as the destruction proceeds to take control on the outside.

No fear, no sorrow, no pain, only sheer tears of joy continuously stain our face as our eyes focus on the scene that lay before us.

Living vegetation ripples the scene leading our eyes to our new home. Across the illustrious green fields lay villas, many mansions of unknown colors of royalty, the walls of which exuded materials of LIFE; buildings, not made by hands, but spoken into existence by the power of His Word. All fashioned according to the rewards for which we worked. Every window pulsated with the light of His Love, welcoming us home.

~~~~~

"Let not your heart be troubled: ye believe in God, believe also in me. In My Father's house are many mansions..." John 14:1-2

That the Blind Might See

THE GREAT SUPPER

Two thieves sneak in back entry, but are fast paced to leave after a failed attempt at thievery. Out back the world is carrying on as usual, children, addicts, animals, and crime all playing in the alleyways together.

Peering through an opened window in the front, I am aghast at the scene, all of creation spinning around the humble house, faster and faster, once, twice up to eight times over. I fall to my knees for the reel of it, but humble house does not spin. Turning around the back alley, friends are all oblivious to what is transpiring.

Suddenly the spinning top stops. Somewhere inside the over growth of foliage in the front, the sound of a gazillion birds are stirring; unseen birds, but not unheard, birds of every sort, awaiting the great feast, the feast of kings and of captains and of mighty men. They have gathered at His will and now they await the call of the Master, at His will.

~~~~~

"... Come and gather yourselves together unto the supper of the great God; That ye may eat the flesh of kings, and the flesh of captains, and the flesh of mighty men, and the flesh of horses, and of them that sit on them, and the flesh of all men, both free and bond, both small and great."

Revelations 19:17-18

HEAT WAVE

Surveying the scene, I'm standing on the cement ground; the destitute atmosphere deadens the color of the towering parched trees to my left. I hear voices of fear in the near distance, and moaning, nothing is stirring except a slight breeze. Overhead incoming from the west side of the sky is an eerie encroaching darkness, and to the east is fading light. Somewhere emanating from the window to a house in the rear is a radio blaring the 149 degree temperature which will soon translate to 199, but my skin only registers a 72 degree day. Why?

The wind begins to howl and become hurricane force in strength. A storm door begins to bang profusely against the house, caught up in the turmoil of the winds fury. We must get to safety now. "It's time," a voice gently whispers, "It's time".

~~~~~

"And the Fourth angel poured out his vial upon the sun; and power was given unto him to scorch men with fire. And men were scorched with great heat, and blasphemed the name of God, which had power over these plagues; and they repented not to give Him Glory."
Revelation 16:8-9

GATEWAY TO HEAVEN

And a window was opened; an eight foot tall window was opened to me. The darkness is almost complete but I can still see; the world is below me and the sky expands above me.

"Can you see them?" echoes an envoy's voice by my side.

"Can you see them?"

Darts of light are edging just beyond realms of my eyes in the sky.

"Lord, open her eyes that she may see," implores the envoy by my side. Immediately the impediment of my eyesight has vanished, and there fulfilling the Living Word, in the vastness of the heavens were angelic beings of the Most High; all arranged in groups of threes, each surrounding the gateway to Heaven.

Yes, Yes, My God Yes, I can see them. Ready and prepared for the voice of the trumpet, every one made of unearthly light and filling the skies with indescribable beauty.

"They are all there at the commandment of the Great King!" The envoy cries. "They, we don't know at what hour, but we know the time draws nigh."

There they stood like a grand display of majestic holiness, waiting to roll back the sky, waiting to snatch "the ready" from the confines of a sin cursed habitation and escort us, "the bride" into the awaiting loving arms of her Christ. And so shall we ever be with the Lord!

That the Blind Might See

SAFETY

Panting, running, many footsteps can be heard in the darkness. Fear and terror is registering in the air, quiet grief and panic is the framework of mayhem. Abandoned high-rises silhouette the midnight sky but even the tons of iron and metal cannot provide safety—But from what?

A quiet, urgent, unspoken voice echoes into the darkness, *72 warheads are overshadowing this land of the free and on distant shores of time, seeking out their prey these pompous spirits bewitching the souls of men.*

"Shush," someone whispers. "We must find safety; we must seek refuge."

Suddenly just a burst of light pierces the darkness in a not so distant place, a place just within reach of hope.

"Come follow me to safety!" I cry. "Do not despair." Pleading and keeping watch on that emblem of hope, trunk so wide there was no encompassing it; its two humongous branches reaching into the heavenlies and oh the living leaves made of light reflecting its healing green colors, while sparkles of gold played at the tips, beckoning for all to come.

~~~~~

"In the midst of the street of it, and either side of the river, was there The Tree of Life", which bear twelve manners of fruits, and yielded her fruit every month; and the leaves of the Tree were for the healing of the nations." Revelation 22:2

Since having this dream, I have now learned that there are ones of the mayan culture that have compassed this land opening up 72 gateways or portals of hell located throughout this country using the mysterious crystal skulls. These gateways are, I believe, the 72 warheads that compassed this land in the dreams. For these warheads or heads of war of satan will, as the scripture has said, in the book of Revelation "and it was given unto him to make war with the saints…." But Jesus said "…upon this Rock I will build My Church, and the gates of hell shall not prevail against It."

Now I hear the master saying the tree that I saw, this is the TREE of LIFE, THIS IS CHRIST! As it was in the beginning so is it now! The Choice must be made! The Church, yes, I said the Church, because in Revelation, it says to the Church at Laodicea! Yes the tree of the knowledge of good and evil is so ingested by the church that it had literally become a part of the church, which is why it is so blind and wretched and naked. Yes, that Laodicean Church was once just like Adam before the fall—sinless! Because Christ had washed away their sins! But then they chose to try to become *like gods*, instead of becoming the sons of God. So because they believed the lie that they would not surely die, they died! **Oh that the Blind might see!**

REPENTANCE

A deadening field lay before me beneath a foreboding sky. Standing in the doorway, the air was so thick with expectation that I could almost taste fear. From the sky strange streaks began to fall upon the ground, *Oh my God its fire,=; it's raining down fire.*

I reach down to touch the flame sputtering on the ground, but I do not feel the heat of the flame; it bears no effect on me. Out of the corner of my eye to the right, hovering just above the rooftop, witchcraft, idolatry and vehement spirits are jaunting up out of this unrecognizable dilapidated house.

Repulsion began to grip my being, as my eyes began to register names of blasphemy graffitied all over this house as it daunted about like an irritating pestering insect. There before my unsuspecting eyes in huge letters, in a stamp like fashion, were the words written "the house of God". My mind repelling the thought, as my equilibrium began to give way. Before I could fully recover from this horrific scene, a clown like figure began to approach me. Upon closer view I saw it was a court jester.

Peering through disdainful eyes, he looked up at the daunting house and back at me again, and speaking with that unspoken voice he relayed to me that he was "the church."

My world turned into great heaves of repulsiveness but that Holy Sweet still small voice began to soothe my soul and calm my fears. He reigned down peace upon my soul as He began to entrust these words to me.

"The house of God has changed the Truth of God into a Lie. And they worship the creature more than I the Creator," saith the Lord.

"The three prevailing spirits are the spirit of witchcraft, through disobedience and rebellion against the Truth. The spirit of idolatry, they have fashioned themselves like the world. And wickedness is the way of life."

The voice that sounds like many waters began to speak to me saying,

"The church has become an entertainment center; that is what a court jester is, entertainment for hire."

"The church has taken on a male spirit, in that it has taken control, rather than The Almighty being in control."

Pleading and reproving, sorrowful but yet angry, The One that kills and make alive, The One that wounds and heals, The One that was slain from the foundation of the world, spoke audibly and loudly.

"Clothes, and money and cars and homes and disobedience," He said. The sorrow of the Lord impressed upon me with every Spoken Word, so much so that repentance began to flood my total being. I was quite overtaken by the enormity of what the Lord was revealing to my soul.

Overhead, one by one these things, these idolatrous things, were paraded before me.

"Tell them," says the God of Glory, the Omnipotent One. "Tell them I come."

The thunderous voice grows louder as I open my tear stained eyes, the thunderous voice is all around me in my bedroom, in my being, all around the house, the very walls are trembling and humbling themselves before His Presence.

"I come. Tell them my reward is with me. They have given heed to seducing spirits and doctrines of devils. Blessed and Holy is He that keeps his garment, that he may not be found naked."

THAT THE BLIND MIGHT SEE

"Let Us Hear the Conclusion of the Matter"

THAT THE BLIND MIGHT SEE

But, We who are the Royal Seed, A Royal Priesthood, through Christ Jesus Our Lord, have ears to hear what the Spirit is saying to the Church. We are hearing the sound of the raging thunder and we are counting the number of bell tolls in this midnight hour. We hear the earth cry out, as the labor pangs come even closer. We are the Church of Philadelphia!

Let the hell hounds rage, let the demons howl, but if you look very close, through the spiritual eye, you will see that they limp a hurting from the weights of heavy chains that are controlled by none other than the God of Glory Himself. They can't say no more than The Master will allow. They can't come no further than the Saviour will forebear. They can't do anymore to us then The God of Glory will give them permission to do. For Our Lord will not allow no more on us then we can bear. And whatever

He allows is because He knows we have what it takes to handle it. Just as He was bragging on Job, so is He bragging on us who are doing His will.

God's Church is victorious and is not contained under one building or under one organization. Yes, they must all be Holy and follow the Apostles' doctrine, Baptized in Jesus' name and filled with the Holy Ghost, speaking in other tongues as the Spirit of God gives utterance. They also must be walking in obedience and in the Truth.

Most churches as a whole have given into the lie and have all kinds of thievery disguised as services for the Lord. But we live in this day where God said He will take a people out of a people.

God's people must beware. There are wolves in sheep clothing among us and the wolves in wolves clothing, they are there to devour the sheep. They come boldly in and implant new ideologies by twisting the Word. They sow discord amongst the brethren, they are heady and high-minded, and they love to take the upmost seat in the house. They love exalting titles and positions. They prey on the just and Spiritual by forbidding them to restore ones overtaken in a fault. These so called leaders allow sin to fester and breed into all kinds of malignancies that eat away at the people in the form of idolatry and worldliness, homosexuality, fornications, adultery, and whoremongering.

They use the Scriptures craftily for their own ill-gotten games and are greedy for filthy lucre. Anybody who is doing all kinds of ministries and yet not living holy and doing what's right in God's eyes are all wolves in sheep's clothing.

"Many in the latter days shall depart from the faith having itching ears giving heed to seducing spirits and doctrines of devils." However, God's Church is the victorious Church and it is alive and well, for the Lord never has left Himself without a witness.

From the African Jungle, down into the Amazon's rain, from the hidden places of China their voices are heard on high. Yes, even from the ghettos of the American Urban jungle to fruited plains of Georgia, God's Church is holding fast and holding out until Our Saviour carries us home.

We refuse to bow to baal; we refuse to eat of the forbidden fruit no matter how often we are tempted. We will forever choose to eat of the Tree of Life that Christ's death and resurrection has brought us back to.

We of the second man Adam have our Father's blood coursing through our veins and we cannot help but be obedient because His seed is in us. We are the Bride of Christ; we are bone of His Bone and Flesh of His Flesh.

Just like God took the rib from Adam in the beginning and made Eve (woman), He (Christ) **"Be"** (all there is or ever will be) drew us from His wounded side, through his Blood, and made His Bride. And we have been sent into all the world to be a light to seek and save, like Christ, that which was lost.

We are missionaries and evangelists and pastors and teachers and prophets all ordained by the Living God, all promoted by God not man. For promotion does not come from the east or west or south but from God.

We may or may not even be recognized by man in our respective places but that's okay because we operate under the Authority of the Living God. We are The Body of Christ and members in particular. The Scripture says "**God hath set** (not man) some in the Church, first Apostles, secondarily Prophets, thirdly Teachers, after that, miracles, then gifts of healing, helps, governments, diversities of tongues."   I Corinthians 12:28

"And He gave *some* Apostles; and *some*, Prophets; and *some*, Evangelists; and *some* Pastors and Teachers;" Ephesians 4:11

"God didn't tell us to build all these buildings and do all these other things, He just told us to go and preach the Gospel to every creature."

God's Last will and New Testament was that not any should perish but that all should come to repentance. This is why it is so important that we spread the Gospel. This is why it is so important for all to operate in the ministry that God has given each of us!

You remember that dream or vision that the Lord gave me, whereas The Lord gave me this pure white linen cloth with the cotton seed that had already started to blossom and how He told me to cast it on this body of water I saw before me, and how when I cast it instead of one seed, it became a multitude of seeds, and some fell on mud, some fell in muddy water and some feel in the water? Well, just like in the vision, this seed of righteousness will not be heeded by every ear. Just like in the dream only some will heed the call to God's righteousness, His righteousness! For that Pure white linen cloth stood for the righteousness of God with which He clothes the saints, and we who are the people of God must allow this seed to take root in our soul. But God has showed me some will hear and some will forbear!

But nevertheless the foundation of God stands sure having this seal the Lord knows them that are His.

While standing on the restless shores of this Life, seeing the relentless waves of change, driven by the winds of doctrine, thrashing against the sands of time, I am beginning to see the dawn of eternity.

The night is far spent, and the Day is at hand, we must stand, holding up that all too important Standard of Holiness, until the last grain of sand, in the hourglass of time falls silent and The Great Eternal Wonder clothes us with eternity. For the Pathway is certain and my God, the signs are all too clear, and the saving of souls is the reason why Our Lord came to this world, to seek and to save that which was lost!

The Lord in His infinite wisdom has sent these dreams to testify of what has and what is, and what will come to pass. He never leaves Himself without a witness. I only hope and pray that your eyes may be opened by the Spirit of the Living God, so you will not be in the dark and be ignorant of satan's devices.

May the sweet communion of the Holy Ghost rest, RULE, and abide with us, now, henceforth and forever more!

"He that hath an **ear, let him hear** what the Spirit saith unto the churches;" Revelation 2:7

"And the Spirit and the Bride say, Come. And let him that heareth say, Come. And let him that is athirst come. And whosoever will, let him take the Water of Life freely."

Revelation 22:17

THAT THE BLIND MIGHT SEE

In loving memory of our family historian

I love and miss you dearly

Viola Scott Coleman

In loving memory of the preacher

I love and miss you dearly

Bishop Sandy Alexander Coleman

In loving memory of my sweet sister in Christ

I love and miss you dearly

Delores Boone

In loving memory of the standard of Holiness

I love and miss you dearly

Lillian Jones McBride

In loving memory of two spiritual giants

I love and miss you both so much

John and Ermma Reid

In loving memory of a praiser

THAT THE BLIND MIGHT SEE

I love and miss you dearly

Naomi Baker

See yall all in that Great gett'n up

Morning!

www.ingramcontent.com/pod-product-compliance
Lightning Source LLC
Chambersburg PA
CBHW032133090426
42743CB00007B/578